Find Your Purpose in Life

Live Each Day with Passion and Clarity

GREGORY L. JANTZ, PHD
WITH KEITH WALL

AspirePress

Find Your Purpose in Life:
Live Each Day with Passion and Clarity
Copyright © 2023 Gregory L. Jantz
Published by Aspire Press
An imprint of Tyndale House Ministries
Carol Stream, Illinois
www.hendricksonrose.com

ISBN: 978-1-64938-043-2

Printed in the United States of America
010922VP

Contents

The Key *to a* Satisfying Life

Perhaps you've heard it said that the two most important days in a person's life are the day they were born and the day they discover why they were born.

It's an exhilarating process to discover your purpose in life—why you were born. Almost everyone knows the day they were born, and they celebrate it every year. But many people never discover *why* they were put on earth at this point in time. They drift from one opportunity to another, one situation to another, without a clear sense of direction or focus.

Nearly all of us have asked ourselves, "What am I doing with my life? What is my reason for existing? How can I live with meaning and significance?" Some people are easily able to answer these questions and enjoy a life guided and motivated by a compelling purpose. Many others, however, struggle with these questions for years and never discover their God-given calling.

The truth is, if you want to be content, it's essential to discover your passion. Without a clear purpose to guide you, all your activity and ambitions will not ultimately bring fulfillment.

Before we go any further, I want to set the foundation by sharing truths that I believe with absolute conviction:

- You have a mission and a calling. Your life has meaning because you were born for a particular "why"—an indispensable reason for being on earth.

- You were created with God-given talents and skills to live out your purpose.

- You can live a fully energized life, knowing you are contributing significantly to the people closest to you and the larger world around you.

- You have enough and are enough to reach your full potential and become the person God intends you to be.

With these truths in mind, let me ask you: Have you determined your purpose—your *why*—for being on Planet Earth? If it is just to "enjoy the ride," then it won't really matter much what you do with your life. You'll just coast along, hoping things will somehow work out. Or if you want to become wealthy or have status, you'll make it your ambition to climb the career ladder—whether or not it represents your true calling.

On the other hand, when you believe that God created you with a unique purpose, you'll want to know how to live out that mission consistently and effectively. If you have any doubt that your life has meaning, let these words from Scripture sink into your heart and mind: "We are God's handiwork, created in Christ Jesus to do good works, which God prepared in advance for us to do" (Ephesians 2:10). A different translation uses this language: "We are God's masterpiece. He has created us anew in Christ Jesus, so we can do the good things he planned for us long ago" (NLT).

WITHOUT A CLEAR PURPOSE TO GUIDE YOU, ALL YOUR ACTIVITY AND AMBITIONS WILL NOT ULTIMATELY BRING FULFILLMENT.

When you seek to align your thoughts with God's will, you'll begin to recognize his calling for your life and the way he equipped you to fulfill it. You are his "handiwork" and "masterpiece," fully equipped to carry out the plans he has for your life. Living with purpose, direction, and conviction means that you won't wonder where time has gone, regret missed opportunities, or question what your life has amounted to.

Let me share another encouraging Scripture passage, one of my all-time favorites and the theme for the Seattle-based mental health program I founded, The Center: A Place of Hope. The Old Testament prophet Jeremiah spoke this message from the Lord: "'I know the plans I have for you,' declares the LORD, 'plans to prosper you and not to harm you, plans to give you hope and a future'" (Jeremiah 29:11).

Though recorded centuries ago, these words are just as relevant today. God does indeed have plans for you and me. Clarifying our purpose enables us to envision a joyful, gratifying, hope-filled future. We can wake up each morning with enthusiasm and energy for the day ahead, and we can go to sleep each night with the satisfaction of knowing we used our gifts to enrich others.

A clear sense of purpose creates meaning in your life that guides your daily decisions, influences your behavior, shapes your goals, and inspires you to service. In the pages ahead, we'll explore these areas, looking closely at …

- **The power of purpose.** You'll discover the many ways a clear direction in life will benefit you—and others.

- **The many pathways of purpose.** For some people, purpose is focused solely on their vocation—meaningful, satisfying work. But a wholistic perspective recognizes that purpose applies to many aspects of life, including family relationships, friendships, community involvement, spiritual pursuits, and creative endeavors.

- **How to find your purpose.** We'll ask probing questions and discuss specific steps you can take to fuel your imagination and pinpoint your path forward.

At the end, we've included an additional set of activities and exercises to sharpen your focus and set a new trajectory. The goal is not to overhaul your life overnight, but to foster, hone, and update your sense of purpose little by little.

You have come to this book seeking help in finding your purpose—or to update your purpose as you enter a new season filled with fresh challenges and opportunities. Consider me your guide, supporter, and cheerleader as you create a vision for an inspiring adventure ahead.

CHAPTER 1

The Power *of* Purpose

Darla came to The Center at the urging of her two grown children, who knew she had been battling clinical depression for several years. And a fierce battle it had been!

Like most people struggling with deep depression, Darla had endured low energy, insomnia, and lack of motivation for the pursuits that previously brought her joy. By her own admission, she had been *existing* but not really *living* for a long time.

Complicating matters, for twelve years Darla had been raising her son and daughter completely on her own, ever since her husband had walked out and abruptly filed for divorce. He had often neglected to make child-custody payments, forcing Darla to become the primary breadwinner for her family. She served as a cook, house cleaner, tutor, coach, taxi driver, and confidant for her children. What's more, for several years Darla was driving forty-five minutes each way to help her elderly parents, who suffered from chronic ailments.

Then there was her work. As a full-time executive assistant to the vice president of technology for a large software company, her role meant managing dozens of details, including her boss's schedule, correspondence, presentations, and reports. Worse, her boss was eager to make demands and dispense criticisms, but reluctant to offer compliments and encouragement.

"I felt like I was continually babysitting this man," she told me. "He had a brilliant mind for technology, but practically no organizational or people skills. I stuck with that job for eight years because it paid well and came with great benefits. I had the expenses of raising kids and rent to pay, so I made a decision to gut it out. I felt constantly frazzled and miserable."

No wonder Darla ended up exhausted and depleted! Human beings can bear heavy burdens for short periods of time, but when those burdens are present every day, year after year, something has to give. You might be able to lug a two-hundred-pound backpack up a small hill and make it. But if you carry that weight up the side of mountain, eventually your knees are going to buckle and you're going to collapse.

When Darla's youngest child went off to college, she finally had the time and resources to take care of herself and focus on her own wellbeing. With help from my team at The Center, Darla began to recover: She started to process her anger and embittered feelings (especially toward her ex) that had festered for years; improved her nutrition; developed a sleep routine to achieve ample rest; established an exercise regimen; reconnected with her spiritual life; renewed friendships that had waned; and discovered new pursuits that would bring happiness. Ultimately—and most importantly—Darla found renewed purpose in life.

For years, Darla's number one purpose had been to singlehandedly raise two kids—at the same time she was caring for elderly parents and striving to be a responsible

employee at a high-stress job. Now, with both kids grown, it was Darla's turn to think about her future. She began brainstorming and dreaming about the kind of life that would help her feel energized and alive.

By the time she finished her treatment program, Darla had begun answering questions and completing exercises to help clarify her path forward. I knew that recovering from depression and regaining her sense of purpose would require time, since there are no magic formulas or quick fixes for either challenge. But I was confident Darla was taking solid steps toward a healthy, bright future.

Now fast-forward one year later, when Darla stopped in to share an update. Besides maintaining all the healthy practices she had learned for replenishing her body, mind, and spirit, she had made the bold choice to quit her stressful job with the software company and pursue one that brought more satisfaction.

"I am now the assistant director for a nonprofit that serves low-income single mothers and their children," she told us. "Many of these mothers are from domestic-abuse situations or other painful circumstances, and these courageous women are trying hard to rebuild their lives. They want to create a stable, hopeful situation for themselves and their children."

Darla comes alongside these women to find community resources for housing, food assistance, legal aid, employment, and more. Most important, she has daily opportunities to offer encouragement and support to struggling families.

"Even though my title is assistant director, I like to think of myself as the CEO: Chief Encouragement Officer. God is using my years as an overwhelmed single mother, and my journey through depression, to empathize with these hurting women and to help them in practical ways."

Darla shared that she took a significant salary reduction for her current role, but added, "The pay cut wasn't easy at first, but now it really doesn't matter because my life is so much richer in so many ways."

She concluded her update with sincerity in her voice. "I found my purpose after trudging through life for years. As I left the office last Friday night, I stopped and said a prayer of gratitude: 'Thank you, God, for leading me to this place and this situation. I have never felt so fulfilled in my life. And I have never felt so grateful.'"

■ ■ ■

Too often, we live our lives feeling like spectators instead of active participants with the power to choose our own course. We get caught up in life's flow, whether it's good, bad, or neutral. Wherever the currents take us, that's the direction we go. It's as though we are navigating on autopilot, aimless and adrift.

This is a classic *whatever* approach to life—"whatever happens, happens"—and it may be uncomfortably familiar to you. The *whatever* mode lets life happen to and around you, come what may. Time passes quickly and, before you realize it, you catch yourself wondering, *What have I been doing? What have I accomplished?* As you look back over your life to date, have you lacked a general target, an inspirational *why* that brings you joy and fuels you to better yourself and your world?

IT'S TIME TO TAKE CONTROL AND ACTIVELY AND INTENTIONALLY PARTICIPATE IN THE COURSE OF YOUR LIFE.

Without a clear *why*—your driving passion and the reason for getting up in the morning—you will continue to live like an archer who is shooting at nothing in particular, firing one arrow after another that randomly lands wherever gravity pulls it to. Unless you take intentional action, chances are that circumstances won't force you to change for the positive. If you go along waiting for some "thing," some event to change your status quo, you'll probably be disappointed. But knowing your *why* will help you grow from a reactive approach to a proactive lifestyle. It's time to take control and actively and intentionally participate in the course of your life.

All of us want to echo Darla's words: "I have never felt so fulfilled in my life. And I have never felt so grateful." We want to sense that we're using our time and talents to the fullest. We want to know we're living in harmony with God's plan for our lives. We want to be assured that the investments we've made in people and pursuits have truly mattered. In other words, we want to know our *why*; we want to find our purpose.

When you discover your purpose, you'll experience the reward of many blessings flowing into your life. In the pages that follow, we'll look at ten benefits of finding your purpose.

1. YOU'LL FIND YOUR CALLING

Many people hear the word *purpose* and think it applies only to grand, world-changing work. Not necessarily. I define purpose as the *one unique thing* we each have to offer, no matter how big or small. It's a matter of investing your gifts and talents to benefit a nation or a neighborhood, a community or a classroom, an entire company or a single child. Finding your purpose leads to your unique calling.

WHAT YOU IDENTIFY AS YOUR PATH WILL BE DIFFERENT FROM THE COURSE THAT OTHERS TAKE.

Your personal purpose may be to raise healthy children or invest in the lives of your grandchildren. It may be to help homeless people get off the streets and back on their feet. It might be to create art that inspires others. Finding a clear sense of purpose will be unique for everyone—and what you identify as your path will be different from the course that others take. What's more, your purpose will likely shift and change throughout life in response to evolving priorities and changing circumstances. The possibilities are endless, and only you can know which one best fits at any particular season of your life.

GETTING STARTED

To begin discovering your unique calling, try this exercise: Look back on your life and identify the situations that brought you the most joy, fulfillment, and gratification. Review your experiences and take note when you hear yourself say, *I absolutely loved doing that!* Then finish the following sentences:

▨ What brings me to life more than anything is

_____.

▨ I never feel more energized than when I

_____.

▨ The number one gift I can give to the world is

_____.

▨ The need that stirs my soul more than any other is

_____.

Finding and following your calling is essential to health and growth. Why? Because it's what keeps you going when you want to give up. It's what renews your energy after an exhausting week. It's what brings joy to your hurting heart.

2. YOU'LL LIVE YOUR OWN STORY

Finding your purpose will inspire you to live as the hero of your own story. Like all stories, yours involves a hero (you), a journey (the battles you've fought), and a prize (lifelong fulfillment). In fact, that progression is found in every story ever told, from ancient myths sung around the fire, to fairy tales, to modern blockbuster films. Embedded in all stories is a blueprint for changing and growing stronger. In other words, struggling is not failing; it's part of being human.

As Joseph Campbell, the great mythologist and author of *Hero with a Thousand Faces*, once wrote, "It is by going down into the abyss that we recover the treasures of life. Where you stumble, there lies your treasure."[1] That's great news. It means you need not look back with regret, but rather with hope that you've arrived at this time in your life stronger and better than ever.

There is yet another universal truth about heroes that you need to know about as you look ahead. The true heroes that we find in books, movies, and real-life stories are never content to passively let events happen to them. When things look dark and all hope seems lost, they refuse to give up or give in. They are tenacious beyond all reason and stubbornly believe in what others say is impossible. They get back up again and again when they're knocked down.

Now that you have chosen to clarify the purpose of your own journey, it's important to dig in your heels and tap into the heroic determination to press onward with fierce resolve. The future is yours. Defend it. Fight for it in the same way that the warriors you admire most would.

3. YOU'LL RECLAIM YOUR DESIRES

It's remarkable that people often have trouble finishing the simple sentence, "I want ..." And I'm not referring to providing lofty, beauty pageant answers like "I want world peace," or vengeful ones such as "I want my sister to suffer for her cruelty!" I'm talking about the ability to express our basic needs and desires. Somehow, the process of growing up teaches most of us to think that what we want out of life is secondary to ... well, just about everything and everyone else.

> DIG IN YOUR HEELS AND TAP INTO THE HEROIC DETERMINATION TO PRESS ONWARD WITH FIERCE RESOLVE.

Sure, there's a time to work hard and sacrifice short-term satisfaction in order to meet our goals. But when that becomes all there is to living, problems arise. Desire is the fuel that refines our purpose and

powers achievement. Without it, there's a hard limit to what we will even try.

Reclaiming your desires is really about remembering what you love. You are allowed to devote yourself to making it happen. That is the essence of finding purpose. Give yourself permission to acknowledge and reach for your desires—and the future will light up in front of you. Getting back in touch with your wants and wishes will empower you to dream again. With renewed knowledge of what brings you joy and rekindled optimism for what lies ahead, you can do away with limiting, sabotaging thoughts, revive old dreams that you abandoned, and create big, bold, new ones.

DESIRE IS THE FUEL THAT REFINES OUR PURPOSE AND POWERS ACHIEVEMENT.

LOOK BACK SO YOU CAN LOOK FORWARD

There is nothing more exciting than realizing that the rest of your life can be what you choose to make it. Yes, unforeseen challenges will always be part of the fabric of life. But they don't have the final say in how you experience the world. That power belongs to you. Here are some tips for tapping into that excitement.

- **Recall your childlike joy.** On a sheet of paper or your electronic device, write the open-ended sentence, "When I was a kid, I loved to _____." List as many different items as you can muster. Then use your imagination to recall every sensation you encountered. How did these activities look, feel, sound, or taste? Write about the experiences in vivid detail. Let yourself be back there again, enjoying life.

- **Dig a little deeper.** Using the list you just made, start a new one by filling in these blanks: "I loved _____ because _____." There are no wrong answers—only the need to be honest. The idea is not just to take a trip down memory lane, but also to revive the freedom to follow your truest desires.

- **Add some new items to your list.** Now that you've started to recall how to think and act like a spontaneous child, let your creativity flow. "Wouldn't it be fun to _____?" "I'd have a deeper sense of meaning if I could _____." "I've always wanted to _____." Don't hold back. Dream big. Pick one of the activities you listed, and start making plans to do it!

- **Cut, print, and paste.** Using pictures you glean from magazines or online, create a collage that depicts your future dreams. You might select images that represent continuing education, good health, financial stability, satisfying relationships, service opportunities, or possessions you can be proud of. Or perhaps you'll include photos of your family, a person whose qualities you admire, or a creative project you want to pursue. Find quotes that inspire you and weave them throughout. When finished, hang your work in a place where you'll see it every day. Let it serve as a reminder of your decision to no longer settle for less than the best in your life.

4. YOU'LL ACTIVATE YOUR IMAGINATION

Here's a startling truth: *Everything* created by human beings—from the first stone wheel to the International Space Station orbiting the earth today—began as a vision formulated in someone's mind. In other words, before we create anything, we must first *see* it.

Go ahead and test that claim for yourself. Try to fold a paper airplane without visualizing its finished shape first, or draw a picture of a rose without thinking about how you'll shape the petals. It's not just difficult; it's also impossible. We are made to imagine, and the world is filled with the results of our imaginings.

So often in life, we fall into ruts and routines that don't bring us joy or a sense of meaning. We settle for the mediocrity of going through the motions instead of imagining, in vivid detail, exactly what we want a brighter future to look like. Do you feel called to a new vocation, one that will offer more opportunities to grow and give? Picture your dream career as clearly as you can. For example, if you feel a desire to volunteer to help needy children, envision yourself among them— interacting, laughing, teaching. Replace the image of yourself as unsatisfied and unenthused with a new one that shows you full of energy and vitality. Your moment-to-moment experience of life will improve when your thoughts are filled with hopeful images, and you will rest assured that things are shifting into place to bring your vision out of your head and into the world.

5. YOUR INNER LIFE WILL GROW

For many people, the topic of finding purpose is focused outward on activities, accomplishments, and careers. That's fine as far as it goes—but it doesn't go quite far enough. I believe purpose involves both an *inward focus* and an *outward focus*. Further, I believe that developing your inward purpose is the more important part of the equation. That's because the important *things you do* will emerge from the qualities that comprise *who you are.*

GOD HAS ALREADY CREATED THE MAP OF YOUR LIFE; HE KNOWS EVERY STEP OF THE WAY BEFORE YOU DO.

As you devote your inner-life purpose to becoming a person of integrity, compassion, and generosity (or whatever qualities are most important to you), your outer-life purpose will inevitably grow out of this effort. Then you will enjoy a wholistic life purpose that draws upon your best inward and outward attributes.

If you're wondering which characteristics to develop, look no further than Scripture for guidance. The apostle

Paul provided a list of inner qualities that will develop as we walk in harmony with God's will for our lives: "The Holy Spirit produces this kind of fruit in our lives: love, joy, peace, patience, kindness, goodness, faithfulness, gentleness, and self-control" (Galatians 5:22–23 NLT).

When you experience these qualities and strive to develop them more and more, you will have the satisfaction of knowing your inner purpose is being fulfilled.

> "WHERE THERE IS NO VISION, THE PEOPLE PERISH."
>
> –Proverbs 29:18 KJV

God has already created the map of your life; he knows every step of the way before you do. He knows what will bring you true inspiration and satisfaction, because he made you—mind, body, spirit, and soul. He also knows that your best path forward is forged by first attending to your inner character.

GUARD YOUR THOUGHTS

The life you experience in your outer world is directly linked to the quality of your inner world—where your internal dialogue shapes the landscape. If you indulge a constant stream of negative and critical thoughts, you are unlikely to feel much joy in living or to inspire it in others. If your inner voice tells you that you'll never achieve your dream, you probably never will.

The apostle Paul has some excellent advice about what to do when negativity barges in: "In every situation, by prayer and petition, with thanksgiving present your requests to God. And the peace of God, which transcends all understanding, will *guard your hearts and minds* in Christ Jesus" (Philippians 4:6–7, emphasis added).

Then he explains how to refocus our thoughts: "Finally brothers and sisters, whatever is noble, whatever is right, whatever is pure, whatever is lovely, whatever is admirable—if anything is excellent or praiseworthy—think about such things. Whatever you have learned or received or heard from me, or seen in me—put it into practice. And the God of peace will be with you" (Philippians 4:8–9).

Pay attention to your mental chatter—and steer it toward gratitude and positive affirmations about yourself and others. You'll be shocked how much more peaceful, joyful, and meaningful your life becomes.

6. YOU'LL MAXIMIZE YOUR GIFTS AND TALENTS

The combination of gifts you have to offer the world originate from what God has already blessed you with—your uniqueness. There is no one else in the entire world just like you.

Scripture makes clear that each of us has been given a distinct combination of gifts that can be used in a variety of roles: "We have different gifts, according to the grace given to each of us. If your gift is prophesying, then prophesy in accordance with your faith; if it is serving, then serve; if it is teaching, then teach; if it is to encourage, then give encouragement; if it is giving, then give generously; if it is to lead, do it diligently; if it is to show mercy, do it cheerfully" (Romans 12:6–8).

A TRUE GIFT IS SOMETHING YOU'RE NOT ONLY SKILLED AT BUT CAN ALSO GIVE BACK TO THE WORLD WITH EASE AND PLEASURE.

In order to discover your gifts and talents, you may need to turn off old messages of inadequacy and imperfection that others have told you or you have told yourself— messages that you aren't good enough, you don't have what it takes, or you don't measure up.

Instead, listen to what God has to say about who you are. He gave you your gifts so you could use them for your own good and the good of others. A true gift is something you're not only skilled at but can also give back to the world with ease and pleasure. You probably already have a long list of things you're good at but don't enjoy doing. When your life and work decisions are based on your gifts and not merely your capabilities, the power of purpose emerges, bringing contentment, energy, and fullness of life.

7. YOU'LL LISTEN MORE CLOSELY TO GOD

Finding purpose compels us to attune our ears to God's voice. I've often thought how nice it would be to literally have God as my navigator, for him to stand right beside me offering directions: "Go this way ... Take this path ... Turn around and go the other way." It would be so much easier if God simply told me my purpose in life and the specific things I'm called to do. It's true that God provides guidance to us when we ask for it. Still, his direction is not always definitive or blatantly clear. Usually I have to listen intently in order to hear his voice and understand his directions. Sometimes it takes work and effort to put myself in a position where I can hear God, but nothing can compare with knowing I'm where he wants me.

Show me your ways, Lord,
teach me your paths.

Guide me into your truth and teach me,
for you are God my Savior,
and my hope is in you all day long.

—David's prayer in Psalm 25:4–5

8. YOU'LL DRAW UPON YOUR OPTIMISM

By its very nature, finding purpose leads us to anticipate a future outcome. An optimist expects it will be positive; a pessimist presumes it will be negative. An optimist hopes for the best, but a pessimist fears the worst. Hope and fear battle in your heart for supremacy, but if you want to live with purpose, it's essential that the hopeful optimist inside of you wins.

I appreciate the words of Jane Ollis, former chair of Kent Institute of Directors: "Optimism draws you into the future. It puts you in the right space to create compelling purposeful visions, how to achieve them and then, the icing on the cake, it supplies you with the positive energy and drive you need to deliver them. Like a gentle wind pushing you from behind it steers you around obstacles as they appear in your path and keep you focused on where you are heading."[2]

IF YOU WANT TO LIVE WITH PURPOSE, IT'S ESSENTIAL THAT THE HOPEFUL OPTIMIST INSIDE OF YOU WINS.

Optimism is not a matter of wishful thinking or unrealistic idealism; it is a choice to believe that the most positive outcome will occur in any situation, despite overwhelming evidence to the contrary. An optimist will cling to the anchor of hope when the winds of despair buffet and blow. And when the storm is over, the optimist will still be standing in hope and living with purpose.

TEN WAYS TO CULTIVATE AN OPTIMISTIC OUTLOOK

Researchers have long understood that a person's attitude largely determines his or her success in their career, relationships, athletic pursuits, financial goals, and other areas of life. If you are a pessimist by nature, it's possible to make changes and form habits that will shift your thinking to the positive end of the spectrum. Here are some ways to boost your positive outlook and move yourself closer to your purpose in life.

1. **Don't let tomorrow spoil today.** Worrying about tomorrow's troubles—which may or may not happen—steals your happiness in the present moment. Focus on today, and trust Jesus's promise that "tomorrow will take care of itself" (Matthew 6:34 CEV).

2. **Affirm others often.** Be generous with your compliments. By helping others feel good about themselves, you'll feel better about yourself too.

3. **Affirm yourself often.** Giving yourself compliments throughout the day will provide a boost to your self-confidence. On days when it's hard to feel positive, reward yourself for even the smallest of accomplishments.

4. **Learn from the past, but don't be anchored by it.** You can't change anything about your history, but you can influence your future by working through hurts that hold you back.

5. **Play the hand you've been dealt.** Pessimists spend a lot of time and energy complaining about how the deck is stacked against them; optimists devise the best strategy for the cards they currently hold.

6. **Pay attention to your thoughts.** You control what goes on in your mind. Be quick to reframe negative messages by steering them toward hopeful expectations. Remember that your thoughts can also affect your words.

7. **Be mindful of what you say.** Your thoughts are like arrows made of positive or negative intentions, and your words are the bow that fires them off into the world. Aim to create an optimistic atmosphere by resisting the temptation to speak negatively and releasing positive words instead.

8. **Practice healthy habits.** No one denies the link between physical and emotional well-being. Regular exercise and good nutrition go a long way toward promoting a positive attitude.

9. **Make sleep a priority.** Few things sabotage a positive attitude like sleep deprivation. Ample rest helps you feel more energetic and alert.

10. **Surround yourself with optimistic allies.** Optimism is contagious, so make an effort to spend time with encouraging people who can keep you from drifting negative.

9. YOU'LL DISCOVER POSITIVE HEALTH EFFECTS

Having a strong sense of purpose not only bolsters your self-esteem and fortifies your spiritual life but also promotes physical well-being. Scientific research shows that having purpose can help you …

- **Live longer.** A study of more than seventy-three thousand Japanese men and women found that those who had a strong connection to their sense of purpose tended to live longer than those who didn't.[3] Additionally, in his study of "Blue Zones" (geographical areas where people tend to live longer), author and researcher Dan Buettner identified a strong sense of purpose as a common quality among centenarians.[4] In 2014, researchers studied data gleaned from tracking adults over

a fourteen-year period and found that "having a purpose in life appears to widely buffer against mortality risk across the adult years."[5]

■ **Deal more effectively with pain.** Purpose can also positively affect pain management. A study in the *Journal of Pain* found that women with a strong sense of purpose were better able to withstand heat and cold stimuli.[6]

■ **Prevent Alzheimer's disease.** Researchers at the Rush Alzheimer's Disease Center in Chicago found that elderly people who felt a low sense of life purpose were more likely to suffer from Alzheimer's disease than those with a strong purpose.[7]

10. YOU'LL MAKE THE MOST OF EACH DAY

In 2005, Steve Jobs delivered perhaps the most memorable commencement speech ever given at Stanford University. He shared stories from his life that helped shape and define who he became as a person and innovator. When he was seventeen years old, Jobs read a quote that went something like this: "If you live each day as if it were your last, then someday you'll most certainly be right." As he explained to his audience, "It made an impression on me, and since then, for the past thirty-three years, I've looked in the mirror every morning and asked myself, 'If today were the last day of my life, would I want to do what I am about to do today?' And whenever the answer has been no for too many days in a row, I know I need to change something."[8]

The quote Jobs shared drives home the point that each of us is given a certain number of days to walk the earth—to love, learn, give, and receive. Scripture tells us, "A person's days are determined; you [God] have decreed the number of his months and have set limits he cannot exceed" (Job 14:5). God knows the number of our days, but we don't. We only know for sure that they are not infinite.

This idea should not be depressing to us, but should instead motivate and inspire us to make the most of each day. If you are searching for your purpose in life, you know what it feels like to have days when you feel blah, gray, and ho-hum. You know what it's like to be busy with many good and productive things—but still wonder whether those activities represent your unique calling.

There are plenty of demands and distractions that consume our time and pull our focus from our top priorities. We must remember that we're the ones who decide whether to allow them to affect and impact us. We also can't waste our tomorrows ruminating about our yesterdays. And we shouldn't spend our precious todays anticipating negative things that might happen, especially when there is so much promise and potential in the present moment.

The psalmist asked of God, "Teach us to number our days, that we may gain a heart of wisdom" (Psalm 90:12). Finding purpose is all about gaining a heart of wisdom so we can invest our time with intentionality and foresight.

■ ■ ■

One thing we know for sure from this brief survey of the benefits of purposeful living is that it enriches our lives in numerous ways. In the next chapter, we'll look at the various aspects of your life that purpose will influence for the positive.

"AS EACH HAS RECEIVED A GIFT, USE IT TO SERVE ONE ANOTHER, AS GOOD STEWARDS OF GOD'S VARIED GRACE: WHOEVER SPEAKS, AS ONE WHO SPEAKS ORACLES OF GOD; WHOEVER SERVES, AS ONE WHO SERVES BY THE STRENGTH THAT GOD SUPPLIES—IN ORDER THAT IN EVERYTHING GOD MAY BE GLORIFIED THROUGH JESUS CHRIST."

—1 Peter 4:10-11

CHAPTER 2

The Many Pathways of Purpose

In his book *Wishful Thinking*, theologian Frederick Buechner elegantly states his view on calling like this: "The place God calls you to is the place where your deep gladness and the world's deep hunger meet."[9]

Here, Buechner beautifully marries our individual desires to our call to selflessness and service. To put it another way, Buechner hints at the importance of both our inner purpose and outer purpose, as we discussed in the previous chapter. One of the primary tasks of life is working out how to integrate the two.

Just as we all have an inner purpose (who we are) and an outer purpose (what we do), we also have a variety of situations and opportunities that deserve our careful consideration. Each of us has a multifaceted life, with family relationships to keep strong, finances to manage, social issues we are concerned about, hobbies we enjoy, and so much more.

In this chapter, I want to nudge you to expand your perspective of purpose beyond your career, so that it includes other aspects of your life that are dear to you. Your work matters greatly, but you are much more than your job. Each part of your life is important enough for you to invest your passion.

To move us along on the journey, let's explore five different areas where your purpose can and should be applied.

✝ 1. SPIRITUAL PURPOSE

We can't talk about purpose without talking about the one who made all things. If you're like most people, you have probably lain in bed at night wondering if you're on the right track in life. When this question is looming large in your mind, it can be hard to believe that God really has a plan for your life. After all, if he did, wouldn't he have made it perfectly clear?

Yet throughout Scripture, God reiterates time and again that he cares about nations and individuals alike. We read stories of downtrodden people raised up by God to fulfill his purposes. One example is the message God gave to his people through the prophet Ezekiel. At that time in biblical history, God's people were exiled from their homes, taken captive in faraway lands. They were saying, "Our bones are dried up and our hope is gone; we are cut off" (Ezekiel 37:11). To these downtrodden people, the Lord gave Ezekiel a vision of new life. In this vision, Ezekiel sees a valley filled with dried bones miraculously come together and rise again from the dust. God promised to his exiled people, "I will put breath in you and you will come to life…. I will put my Spirit in you and you will live, and I will settle you in your own land" (Ezekiel 36:6, 14). He didn't tell his people exactly *how* this would happen with all the details they probably wanted to know, but he called them to trust that it *would* happen. And if you continue reading this story, you'll see that God did in fact bring his people back from exile, and they rebuilt their lives in their homeland.

THROUGH THE PEOPLE WE MEET AND SERVE IN OUR PLACES OF WORSHIP, WE DEVELOP A CLEARER VIEW OF OURSELVES.

You might not know precisely how God will work in your life, but you can know this: You are called and equipped by God to be a particular kind of person and to do specific things in the world, and when you seek his will for your life, you can trust in his promise that his Spirit will enable you to accomplish all that he has called you to do.

There are many ways to uncover God's purpose for our lives, but one of the best ways I've found is by connecting to a community of faith. Through the people we meet and serve in our places of worship, we develop a clearer view of ourselves. We learn what motivates us, delights us, annoys us, and challenges us. Proverbs 27:17 proclaims, "As iron sharpens iron, so one person sharpens another." Our hearts and minds are shaped in community. Our character is revealed and reformed that way too. Through a community of faith, we also come into contact with people we may not ordinarily meet. Spiritual communities serve as tools God uses to refine us and prepare us to carry the healing message of God's love to the wounded world. In this way, these places provide us opportunities to grow in our inner purpose and live out our outer purpose.

 ## 2. VOCATIONAL PURPOSE

Over the years, I've enjoyed countless conversations with people about the topic of purpose. These conversations naturally weave in the aspects of family, legacy, vocation, and social impact—areas in which we all want to leave our mark. Invariably, the broader conversation lands on the subject of vocation.

Most people I speak with view their career as the natural expression of their purpose. This is especially true for people in their twenties who are just starting out. Members of the younger generations care deeply about integrating their purpose and professional lives. The logic goes, if you're going to commit roughly one third of your life to work, you may as well ensure that those hours count toward something meaningful.

According to research conducted by LinkedIn, 86 percent of polled Millennials stated they would take a pay cut if it meant working for a company that shared their personal values.[10] Also, a study conducted by Deloitte, a professional services corporation, revealed that younger Millennials "would be more motivated and committed at work if they felt their employer made a positive impact on society."[11]

BY BLENDING YOUR PERSONAL VALUES WITH YOUR OCCUPATION, YOU CAN FIND DEEP SATISFACTION IN YOUR CHOSEN CAREER.

If you're in this stage of life and just starting to consider how your vocation and purpose intersect, I recommend working with a career counselor who can help you identify passions, strengths, work style, and personal values. They'll guide you in learning about occupational opportunities, educational requirements, average salaries, and more. By blending your personal values with your occupation, you can find deep satisfaction in your chosen career.

TAKING INVENTORY

This is a good time to take inventory of your vocational purpose by reflecting on the following questions:

- Does your current job align with your greater purpose in life?

- Does your work allow you to express your character or practice serving others?

- If the answer to the above questions is no, is it possible to infuse your current role with meaningful, life-giving outlets?

- How can you carry out your daily vocational tasks in ways that are unique to you?

- What skills, passions, and ideas do you bring to the table that no one else can?

Same Purpose, Different Location

But what about those who view a job as simply a way to put food on the table, keep a roof over their heads, or put the kids through college? With recent changes in the economy, many people find themselves in this situation—disillusioned and questioning their sense of purpose. In a perfect world, everyone would enjoy rich and meaningful work that brings a sense of fulfillment. But as we all know, this can't always be the case. It can be hard not to despair when your current occupation is less than what you'd hoped for.

I'll never forget Ryan, who was trained as a pastor but found himself working midnight shifts in a warehouse to support his family. The church he led had been struggling to grow—and was hurting financially. The board of elders asked him (or rather told him) to accept a pay cut, significant enough that Ryan concluded he simply could not support his family on such little income.

Ryan shared with me the deep sadness and shame he initially felt when he left the church. "I truly felt called to serve a congregation," he explained. "I couldn't understand why God would call me to spend four years training as a pastor, only to close all the doors to ministry."

Eventually Ryan realized he was behaving as though God had forgotten all about him. He decided that God must have good works prepared for him to do at the warehouse, and it was his challenge to discover and accomplish those tasks. He knew he had an opportunity to practice what he had preached and to believe God still had a plan for him.

"I had a major mindset shift," he recalled. "I came to see the warehouse crew as my new 'congregation.' I kept my purpose of service, encouragement, and care. My *purpose* remained the same, but the *place* I applied it changed."

Ryan committed himself to becoming a reliable team member, and he became better acquainted with his coworkers, serving them however he could. Within the year, Ryan knew the names of their wives and children. He shared in their highs and lows, and he even prayed for and with them. Ryan became known for following through on projects and going above and beyond.

"I actually came to like my job," Ryan said with a smile. "Well, most of the time. It wasn't my dream job, by any means. But I loved the people I worked with, and I had opportunities to care for them every day."

Ryan's authenticity and dedication were refreshing. Even when we don't always love our jobs, it's undeniable that doing something well creates a sense of pride and satisfaction.

After two years of working at the warehouse, Ryan accepted a full-time pastoral position at another church. To hear Ryan speak about it now, it's clear that the two years he spent at the warehouse were not wasted time. He was growing in faithfulness and love. Ryan's story serves as a reminder that no matter where we find ourselves employed, there is always a way to pursue our purpose.

DOING SOMETHING WELL CREATES A SENSE OF PRIDE AND SATISFACTION.

Like Ryan, many of us have taken jobs that are less than satisfying for the sake of making ends meet. And also like Ryan, it's important for us to remember that profession and purpose are not interchangeable. If our sense of purpose is bound to what we do for a living, it's possible we will become discouraged when a disruption in the economy, a cross-country move, or a company reorganization occurs. These external events can threaten to derail our lives, unless we remember that even when our circumstances change, we are never without purpose.

Adapting Your Purpose

Former Boston Red Sox player Mo Vaughn's story is an example of how radically a person's life purpose can change. Baseball fans around the country will recall that in his heyday, Vaughn (known as "The Hit Dog") was unparalleled both on and off the field. In 1995, Vaughn won the American League's Most Valuable Player award thanks to his thirty-nine home runs and .300 batting average. He was on top of his game until 2003, when a knee injury forced him into early retirement. And just like that, it was all over.

Vaughn had spent his life on the field; his mother introduced him to baseball when he was just three years old. It's safe to say that baseball was a major component of his life's purpose. Like many athletes who must retire too soon due to injury, Vaughn was faced with the choice between reliving his glory days or adopting a new goal in life. Vaughn chose the latter and soon started a real estate company, Omni New York LLC, with the purpose of rejuvenating low-income housing in New York City.

In 2017, Vaughn's company was named Developer of the Year by the New York Housing Conference. According to Omni's website, the company has owned and managed seventeen thousand units of affordable housing in eleven states. Though few of us can relate to his level of fame and accomplishment, Vaughn's extraordinary story contains universally relevant lessons.

One way or another, every job comes to an end. There will be a day when you turn off the lights after placing your last sales call, teaching your last class, stitching up your last patient, waiting your last table, or doing whatever it is your job entails—for the final time.

THE OPTIONS FOR SERVING OTHERS ARE ENDLESS, IF ONLY WE HAVE EYES TO SEE THEM.

Vocation is a major expression of purpose, but remember that your biggest contribution to the world isn't merely what you do between 9:00 a.m. and 5:00 p.m. Our careers exist to serve our purpose, not the other way around; there are plenty of good works waiting for us beyond the boundaries of our jobs. We all have neighbors in need, and we all have friends who could use a listening ear. The options for serving others are endless, if only we have eyes to see them.

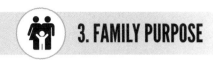

3. FAMILY PURPOSE

Your purpose will change over time, with each new season. It's wise to reevaluate not only *what* God is calling you to do, but *who* God is calling you to serve.

A WISE PERSON WILL NATURALLY UPDATE THEIR SENSE OF PURPOSE WITH EACH NEW LIFE STAGE.

For example, the same man who concentrated on building his career in his early twenties may find himself standing at the altar as he nears the end of that decade, eagerly awaiting his bride-to-be. In that moment, his purpose will change. No longer can he focus singularly on his career. He will need to develop the capacity to invest in both his marriage and his profession. And his purpose will expand once more when he holds each of his newborn babies for the first time; when his children leave to start careers of their own; and again when he retires.

A wise person will naturally update their sense of purpose with each new life stage. Failure to do so can leave those he cares about feeling rejected and dejected.

Young people aren't the only ones who must evaluate and update their sense of purpose. Older adults also face this challenge, as illustrated by a 2021 joint study by Edward Jones and Age Wave. The report detailed the health benefits of purpose and family as retirees navigated the COVID-19 pandemic, stating,

> Many retirees have taken on new roles and responsibilities, such as providing childcare to grandchildren … and providing emotional comfort to family and friends. In return, these stepped-up roles have given retirees a greater sense of purpose and connection.[12]

TRANSFORM YOUR IMPACT

Few questions are as powerful as the ones we ask ourselves about our family relationships. Take some time to ponder the following, and consider journaling your answers:

- How would you describe your purpose when it comes to your family?

- Who in your family could use an extra measure of your love and care?

- How can you use your unique skills and gifts to support a member of your family?

- What are some practical steps you can take to develop your family relationships?

The answers to these questions have the potential to transform the impact you have on your family today and into future generations.

4. CREATIVE PURPOSE

In today's fast-paced, technology-driven society, creative outlets are often seen as optional and frivolous—nice additions to life but ultimately unnecessary. Creativity is encouraged in young children—we seem to realize that music and art foster intelligence and social skills—but as we get older, we're taught to prioritize the more "serious work" of life.

Unfortunately, we're sadly mistaken if we believe that creativity is anything less than vital for our quality of life. After all, we're created in the image of a creative God. Whether your brand of creativity involves painting and dancing or baking and gardening, every form of artistic

expression is its own language, useful for telling stories that people everywhere can identify with.

Finding life purpose and expressing creativity is a two-way street. Engaging in new creative pursuits or rediscovering artistic pursuits that have been put on hold can help you discover your purpose as you exercise your imagination and uncover hidden talents. You're using art as a form of "therapy" for envisioning your future life.

WE'RE SADLY MISTAKEN IF WE BELIEVE THAT CREATIVITY IS ANYTHING LESS THAN VITAL FOR OUR QUALITY OF LIFE.

On the other side of the creative coin, many people affirm that creating art *is* their purpose in life. They realize that creative expression is their calling and contribution to the world.

Creative enterprises reveal our innermost longings, challenge us to better ourselves, and help us make sense of the world around us. You may find it helpful to list your creative interests in your journal, then identify how they foster a sense of purpose in your life.

5. FRIENDSHIP PURPOSE

One of the most powerful and underestimated influences in our lives is friendship. Through our earliest friendships, we learn three pivotal lessons about life: how to ask for and receive help, how to compromise, and how to express our needs. We discover that relationships can be a source of fun, excitement, joy, and care.

THE QUALITY OF OUR FRIENDSHIPS IS A BENCHMARK FOR OUR OVERALL HEALTH AND WELLNESS.

As the years pass, our friendships offer a safe haven from life's storms. There is something almost magical about these no-strings-attached, freely given relationships. Proverbs 17:17 describes it well: "A friend loves at all times, and a brother is born for a time of adversity." A true friend willingly and gladly offers support. Scripture says that love is on display when a person literally or figuratively lays down his life for a friend (John 15:12–13).

These thoughts bring to mind a former counseling client named Gail, whom I met when she was in a crisis following a painful divorce. Gail described the chaos her ex-husband had caused by destroying their shared finances, recklessly spending her hard-earned paychecks and racking up thousands of dollars in debt.

Then Gail went on to share how her ex-husband had actively undermined her self-esteem by picking apart her appearance and talents. Over the course of years, his criticism caused Gail to doubt her own ability to reason and problem-solve. She endured the abuse for more than a decade until the day he spoke negatively about her closest friend.

"The day he started criticizing my friend was the day I realized he was all wrong," Gail explained. "My friend had been so faithful and patient with me. I doubted everything about myself, but I didn't doubt her."

Gail credited her friendship with getting her through the hardest parts of the divorce and its aftermath. Perhaps the most impactful aspect was the way Gail's friend assured her that she was more than a victim. "My friend reminded me that I was once a passionate, lively person, and she made me believe I could be that person again," Gail explained. Gail's story points to several truths about friendship, especially that a good friend sees who you truly are and reminds you of your identity when you forget.

The quality of our friendships is a benchmark for our overall health and wellness. When we start to notice these relationships suffering, we may need to take a step back and ask ourselves if we're pouring too much time and energy into other areas of our lives.

Has work been busier than usual lately? Have family affairs been extraordinarily demanding? It's perfectly normal that the amount of time and energy you can invest into your friendships will fluctuate, but if you notice a pattern of separation emerging, it's time to correct course.

INTENTIONAL FRIENDSHIPS

If you'd like to be more intentional about your friendships, you may find it helpful to complete this sentence:

"My purpose is to be a great friend by _____

_____

_____

_____

[trying to show up at important moments, walking with them through hard times, listening more than talking, offering guidance when asked]."

And as you think about how your friendships and your purpose intersect, consider asking those closest to you what characteristics make you a good friend in their eyes. Their feedback may surprise you!

Together we've explored some of the possible purposes that exist for your spiritual, vocational, and creative pursuits, as well as the relationships you share with family and friends. Becoming more intentional in these areas will enhance your relationship with yourself and others in unexpected ways. We've also discussed how those aspects of your life point to your *overall purpose*, and in the next chapter, we'll explore specific steps you can take to find just that—your True North, your *why* ... your passion. Stay tuned—the best part of the journey is ahead!

"YOU ARE TO WALK IN EVERY PATHWAY THAT THE LORD YOUR GOD COMMANDED YOU, SO THAT LIFE MAY GO WELL FOR YOU, AND SO THAT YOU WILL PROLONG YOUR DAYS IN THE LAND THAT YOU WILL POSSESS."

—Deuteronomy 5:33

CREATE A PERSONAL MISSION STATEMENT

Be encouraged in knowing that your purpose isn't a point on a map that you must find in order to feel accomplished, but rather a destination that will reveal itself as you submit to an ongoing process.

As part of the journey, you may find it helpful to create a one-sentence mission statement for each area of purpose we've explored in this chapter (spiritual, vocational, family, creative, social). As you do so, be sure to include some action items for how you will fulfill your mission. You'll also want to make your mission statement **S.M.A.R.T** (**S**pecific, **M**easurable, **A**chievable, **R**elevant, and **T**ime-Bound). Here are some examples:

- "In this season of life, my purpose for my spirituality is to discover more about God's character. I'll work toward this by (1) reading Scripture three times per week, and (2) joining a small group at my church. I'll know it's time to reevaluate my purpose when my small group ends."

- "In this season of life, my purpose for my marriage is to cultivate deeper trust and connection with my partner. I'll work toward this by taking the following steps with my spouse: (1) having a daily 'talk time' to keep communication open and address any concerns, and (2) attending counseling once per week. I'll know it's time to reevaluate my purpose when we've met our counseling goals."

■ "In this season of life, my purpose for my creativity is to use painting to express my emotions. I'll work toward this by enrolling in a painting class. I'll know it's time to reevaluate my purpose when the class is over and I've gained new art skills."

My Personal Mission Statement:

_____

_____

_____

_____

_____

_____

_____

_____

_____

CHAPTER 3

How *to* Find Your Purpose

One of my favorite *Peanuts* cartoons shows Lucy sitting at her five-cent psychology booth, where Charlie Brown has stopped to ask for advice about life.

Lucy explains that on the cruise ship of life, some people place their deck chairs at the back of the ship to see where they've been, while others place their chairs at the front of the ship so they can see where they're going.

Then, looking at Charlie Brown, Lucy asks which way his chair is facing. Without hesitating, Charlie answers glumly, "I've never been able to get one unfolded."[13]

What about you—have you ever had the disheartening feeling that, everywhere you look, people are living with purpose while you're still fumbling around, trying to get situated?

By now you might be saying, "Okay, I can see the value and importance of having a more defined sense of purpose in key areas. Sure, I want to live up to my potential and make a difference in the world, but my life is already jam-packed. And there's just so much noise—so many distractions clamoring for attention and consuming my time and energy. How do I actually go about finding—and living—my unique purpose?"

If such questions have scrolled across your mind as you've read, you're not alone. Research shows that only around 25 percent of American adults claim to have a clear sense of what makes their lives meaningful.[14] Still, the majority seems to be searching for their life purpose. A recent study by Lifeway Research reported that 57 percent of Americans wonder how they can find more meaning and purpose in life "at least monthly, with more than 1 in 5 saying they consider the question daily (21%) or weekly (21%)."[15]

Since you've read this far, you are serious about the quest for purpose. You're eager to make your days and your life count—for good. You've recognized that the rest of your life can, and should, be the best of your life.

In this chapter, you'll find the tools you need for uncovering your purpose. Put these guidelines to work and live by them, and they'll change your life.

Joel's Journey

In his early sixties, Joel, an empty nester, faced an unexpected layoff. Joel felt adrift. With his children raised and his career possibly over, he was asking himself tough questions: *Now that the kids are grown—and now that I'm without a job—what should I do with the rest of my life? What's my new purpose and mission?*

THE REST OF YOUR LIFE CAN, AND SHOULD, BE THE BEST OF YOUR LIFE.

A healthy purpose was what Joel was after. Yes, he would continue to be a faithful, loving husband to his wife; an encouraging, supportive dad and father-in-law; and a nurturing, fun granddad to his children's children. These resolutions were givens in his life, but he didn't want them to be his sole reasons for existence over the next decades.

Joel was entering a new passage, and it was time to reboot. Beyond family and career, what would become his new purpose? What would be his guiding passion to help him accomplish all that God had in store for the rest of his life?

Over the course of several weeks, with pen and notebook in hand, Joel contemplated several questions and recorded his thoughts. Many of the ideas he wrote down came to him randomly—he wasn't trying to formulate specific, word-perfect answers right away. Often his notes were bullet-point lists, scrawled phrases, questions, or even doodles. There was no hurry. He just kept thinking, praying, deleting, and revising.

WHAT WILL BE YOUR GUIDING PASSION TO HELP YOU ACCOMPLISH ALL THAT GOD HAS IN STORE FOR THE REST OF YOUR LIFE?

What follows are the types of questions Joel pondered, and I can tell you that the process has worked wonders for him. Joel completed this soul-search with an invigorating sense of clarity, and I'm confident that the same can happen for you. That's why I strongly encourage you to use these questions as your own springboard to finding your personal, life-giving why and aligning your other goals and desires with it. And, as Joel did, I want you to do so with pen and notebook in hand.

8 Questions *to* Ask *in* Pursuit *of* Your Purpose

1. God, will you guide me as I plan my future?

Such a prayer for divine guidance is one that we're all encouraged to pray. James 1:5 says, "If any of you lacks wisdom, you should ask God, who gives generously to all without finding fault, and it will be given to you." It's evident from Scripture that God invites us to seek him, to ask him for wisdom to guide our decision-making. He knows us far better than we do, and he knows the future, while we can only guess what will happen.

That's why I suggest a "stillness before strategy" approach to seeking your purpose. Ask God to guide you, then listen quietly. He rarely speaks audibly, but he does whisper to our minds and hearts. When we go to him in humble reverence, he delights in helping us think clearly and calmly, which in turn keeps us aligned with his will and tuned in to the strengths, talents, and desires he's given us.

GOD INVITES US TO SEEK HIM, TO ASK HIM FOR WISDOM TO GUIDE OUR DECISION-MAKING.

Next are some methods for seeking God's presence that I have found helpful in my own life and the lives of those I've counseled.

- **Pray.** This is your conversation with God. When you want to know where he wants you to go or what direction to take to get there, just ask. Many people I know talk to God continually throughout the day. They make themselves aware of his presence and constantly check in with him through prayer. Others find it helpful to designate a special time and place for prayer, one that is quiet and allows for introspection.

- **Quiet your mind.** Try to remain still and focused on a central theme or thought. It allows your mind to open up so that God can speak to you directly. Once you attune your ears to his voice, he will provide insights and instruction.

- **Read the Bible.** Scripture is one of the primary ways God speaks to us, so you can expect God to reveal himself when you open its pages. As you seek to discover your purpose in life, you are sure to find wisdom in God's Word. As the psalmist wrote, "Your word is a lamp for my feet, a light on my path" (Psalm 119:105).

- **Journal.** Keep a notebook or journal close by so you can write down thoughts, prayers, questions, feelings, and the insights God gives you. Writing in a journal will help you process and clarify what you believe God is telling you.

Listen intently. Listening requires us to (1) stop talking, and (2) focus on what the other person is saying. Ecclesiastes 3:7 says there is "a time to be silent and a time to speak." Notice that the silent part comes first. Embrace the opportunity to be quiet and wait for God to speak.

2. What would hindsight tell me someday?

The "Hindsight" exercise lets your imagination take you into the future to identify meaningful aspects of life you should focus on. Here's how it works:

- Close your eyes and breathe slowly.

- In your imagination, envision yourself at age ninety-five, enjoying your backyard patio. The flowers smell sweet, and there's a waft of warm breeze. You realize that each month, each week, and each day is a blessing beyond expectations. You're grateful for such a good, long life.

- As you look back, allow yourself to ponder ... and wonder. Despite all the good memories, do you also feel a hint of melancholy as a tear or two tracks down your cheeks? If so, why?

- It's inevitable that the pace and priorities of everyday living elbowed aside some of your goals and dreams. Do any of the following items describe things you wish you had attempted or pursued—dreams that you postponed until "someday"?

- ☐ Spending time with special people

- ☐ Going to certain places

- ☐ Studying subjects you'd always wanted to know more about

- ☐ Reading more great books

- ☐ Learning or improving a skill or hobby

- ☐ Teaching a class or leading a discussion group

- ☐ Joining an outreach to meet a need in the community, nation, or world

In the sunset of your imagination, if you look back over your life and find yourself thinking, *I only wish I had ...* then perhaps you should move those named desires from the realm of "I wish" to the realm of "I will." Perhaps these are the dreams that are now worthy of your time and energy.

The good news is, this hindsight exercise was just a drill—it's likely that you're not yet ninety-five years old. As you bring yourself back to the present, you gain back all the years between then and now. They're yours to utilize as you wish, to use "on purpose" as you pursue the passions, dreams, and resolutions that you noticed. Take some time now to write about them, think about them, and pray about them.

Among Joel's plentiful notes, two observations stood out to him. First, one of his imagined regrets was putting off his desire to help mentor young men and new fathers at his church. Because of his demanding job over many years, he always felt he didn't have the time. And he questioned whether he had any helpful wisdom to pass along.

But looking back from his imaginary mid-nineties, Joel realized that he indeed could have prioritized the time, and that he could have helped guide and encourage younger men even if he *didn't* have all the answers.

So, back in the present, Joel moved his unfulfilled dream from the "I wish" column to the "I will" column. He decided he would summon his courage, step forward, and volunteer to serve as a mentor. In this new stage of life—with no office to go to every day and possessing hard-earned wisdom from raising his kids—he felt the freedom and confidence to step up to this new challenge.

3. Do I have a grand vision for my life that will refine my purpose?

Vision is the building block of every worthwhile enterprise. Before we can create anything—rewarding family and social relationships, a captivating work of art, or successful business ventures, mentoring programs, or soup kitchens—we have to see the end result clearly in our minds. Our imagination must develop a blueprint of ideas before our hands can turn them into reality. Vision and achievement are inseparable.

WHEN WE DREAM BIG AND SEE OURSELVES ACHIEVING SOMETHING SIGNIFICANT, WE ARE SAYING YES TO GOD AND HIS VISION FOR US.

Vision is necessary not only for grand, large-scale projects and endeavors but also for our everyday lives. We need vision to turn the minor details of our daily existence into a mission—to frame our view of work, and other aspects of life we consider mundane and boring, as opportunities to create change.

The imagery of vision is God's language. Far more often than he uses words, he uses our dreams and our desires to share his plans and inspire us to join in. We want something because he wanted it first. When we dream big and see ourselves achieving something significant, we are saying yes to God and his vision for us.

As a mental health professional, I've observed that most of us have a dream or passion we want to pursue, but it is often vague and undefined. Most of us also have a ready answer when asked what we would do with our lives if money and time were not obstacles. The problem arises when our dreams remain unexamined and underdeveloped. In other words, it's important to have the *right* vision, one we can believe in and trust.

Chances are that the vision for a new endeavor or a new direction is brewing within you. So what are the next steps?

Write down a brief description of your dream. The process of writing out your vision helps to organize your thoughts, clarify your purpose, and refine the scope of your ambitions.

Consider the characteristics of a wise and worthy vision. As Proverbs 22:3 advises, "The prudent see danger and take refuge, but the simple keep going and pay the penalty." Your vision must be …

- **Clear.** Lots of people say things like, "I want to be rich" or "My goal is to be generous" or "I want to help people" or "I want to build a successful business." While these are lofty statements, they unfortunately lack focus. For a vision to be clear, it must be as *specific* as possible. Know exactly what you want to achieve. Having a vague and fuzzy dream is a good way to lose sight of the road before you even get started.

- **Compelling.** Your vision should also be energizing and enticing enough to inspire your imagination and efforts—and even those whom you might need to partner with. Suppose you say to your family, "I want to be more intentional about serving our neighbors." That's okay, but how about something that can fuel the fire of possibilities: "Let's think of two neighbors we can serve and care for this month. There's Miriam, who recently lost her husband of fifty years. And there's Leticia, who's parenting solo while her husband is deployed overseas. We'll take them a meal and offer to help with any house or yard projects." Don't water down your dream. Let it sizzle. When you do, others are irresistibly inspired to get on board and help you with their labor, talents, or resources. Vision is contagious—a characteristic that is vital to getting your dream off the drawing board and into the real world.

- **Calculated.** Plenty of people have pie-in-the-sky ideas, but no way to practically see them put into action. The best vision is accompanied by a *plan* for making it a reality. It may sound contradictory to suggest that your vision should be calculated. We don't want to limit our dreams by getting mired in all the details and constraints, do we? But to live with purpose over the long haul of life requires you to take inventory of your assets *and* your liabilities where your dream is concerned. Give yourself a gift you'll never regret: an honest assessment of your chances for success. Purpose-filled people know what resources they will need and where those resources will come from to accomplish their vision and fulfill their passion.

> VISION IS CONTAGIOUS—A CHARACTERISTIC THAT IS VITAL TO GETTING YOUR DREAM OFF THE DRAWING BOARD AND INTO THE REAL WORLD.

- **Committed.** People who have the commitment to defer gratification because they see a greater future good are the ones who will achieve their goals. The foolish person wastes resources because they're not committed enough to their vision to forego current comfort. When an idea has seized your imagination, go for it with wholehearted determination. As physician and social commentator Richard Swenson says,

> A vision is not an arbitrary string of verbiage constructed to fill a vacant morning at the corporate board retreat. It is the foundation for our thoughts, actions, and values. Therefore it is not enough to have a vision—we must also *live* it.... Reach higher than tomorrow, higher than the basement, higher than your moods, and higher than your appetites. Find transcendence in the kingdom of God and determine to live there—even when it is lonely and even when culture isn't helping. It will be the right decision.[16]

Let your vision inspire your imagination. Then, with the help of trusted advisors, run it through the grid of the four hallmarks mentioned above: Is it *clear*, *compelling*, *calculated*, and *committed*? Insist that it pass this test before you proceed. If you do, you'll know that the ground beneath your feet is solid and secure as you take each new step toward turning your dreamed-of purpose into reality.

4. What are my strengths?

Next, invest some thoughtful time into listing your top-ten strengths—anything from public speaking to working math problems in your head to playing the banjo. Do you write well? Play a sport with agility? Create beautiful paintings? Capture inspiring photographs? How are you at leading a team? Cooking and baking? Interior decorating? Fixing mechanical gadgets? Teaching new concepts to others? Investing and money management?

Ask yourself …

- What am I good at?

- What have other people told me I'm good at?

- What do I love to do?

- When do I feel most engaged with what I am doing?

- What do I do well that brings me the most fulfillment?

- What activities make me feel the most alive?

LET YOUR VISION INSPIRE YOUR IMAGINATION. THEN, WITH THE HELP OF TRUSTED ADVISORS, RUN IT THROUGH THE GRID OF THE FOUR HALLMARKS: IS IT *CLEAR, COMPELLING, CALCULATED,* AND *COMMITTED*?

These are just a few thoughts to get you started. And now is not the time to be modest. If you get stuck, ask family members, friends, and coworkers for ideas: "I'm doing a personal exercise that requires me to list my strengths. Would you be willing to brainstorm with me some things you think I'm good at?"

In addition to mentioning tangible skills, your family members or good friends may also bring up your character qualities. Someone might observe that you're outgoing and friendly, or kind and gentle. Or perhaps you often hear comments like "You're a good listener" or "I admire your patience."

Write down everything that comes to mind and is brought up by others. Then let the input sit. After several days, review your notes and ask yourself, *Based on this list, what are the strengths God has given me? What strengths can I feel confident about using in a positive way in the future?*

Knowing and harnessing your strengths will go a long way in helping you discover your purpose as you make the most of your future.

5. How can I continue learning and growing?

You've learned a lot in your lifetime, including the fact there's still so much to learn! As you plan your future, a commitment to continued learning will nurture a sense of never-ending personal growth and fulfillment.

What subjects have intrigued you that you'd like to study further? What activities or skills would you like to explore, practice, and become adept at? Whet your appetite with the following ideas:

- Learn or improve your proficiency at a recreational activity: tennis, bowling, running, hiking, swimming, skiing—you name it. What have you always wanted to try or improve upon?

- Plant and tend a flower or vegetable garden.

- Tackle that long-procrastinated home-improvement project.

- Take classes to expand your computer skills.

- Start a blog and/or develop a podcast on a topic you're passionate about.

- Research and write your family history.

- Learn a new language by taking a class online or at your community college. It could also be as simple as using a language-learning app on your phone.

- Take an international-cuisine cooking class.

- At least every six months, attend a community seminar on a topic that interests you.

- Go after that undergraduate or graduate degree.

- Ask your pastor, teachers, family, and friends for their opinions on the best books ever written. Compile a list and read one title per month.

- Find a good study Bible and begin to read through it—systematically, including the notes and cross-references.

- Jump into the arts. Take advantage of adult-education classes in photography, painting, drawing, stained glass, sculpture, or woodworking.

- Learn or commit to proficiency in playing a musical instrument.

- What other desires come to mind?

After you've identified what appeals to you on the list above, select and rank the five that are most exciting. These are your "Top Five Strategies for Continuing to Learn and Grow."

Some of these new endeavors may last for only a few weeks. Others, depending on the level of enjoyment and fulfillment they bring, may last months, years, or the rest of your days. You can revise the list anytime your desires and passions shift. Use it to help you gain knowledge and hone your skills—and have fun doing so!

6. What kind of contribution can I make in my community?

If you've already made time to volunteer for helpful causes, you may have discovered a fondness for devoting even more of your time, talent, and treasure to meeting the needs in your community and in the world.

I'm convinced that we all need a way to make a positive difference that we feel passionate about. Mine has been to help people overcome tough issues through face-to-face, whole-person wellness therapy, as well as through speaking and writing. Joel's passion is to help guide and mentor young men. Have you identified yours?

Nothing will give you a greater sense of purpose, mission, and joy than a life-changing, people-helping cause that you can invest yourself in. If you don't know yet how you might serve, see if any of these suggestions kindle a flame within you:

- Offer to lead a small group or teach a class at church.

- Help build a home with Habitat for Humanity or another organization.

- Assist your church maintenance team or office staff during the week.

- Volunteer at your local rescue mission, Salvation Army, Goodwill Industries, or similar outreaches.

- Offer to house-sit or pet-sit for friends who need to get away.

- Deliver meals and good cheer through a program like Meals on Wheels.

- Visit and encourage hospital patients or shut-ins.

- Be a host family for exchange students.

- Help with administrative tasks at blood drives and fund-raisers.

- Do yard work for an ill or disabled friend.

- Take a literacy-training course so you can teach basic English skills to immigrants, or tutor struggling students in your area of expertise.

- Serve as a spiritual mentor and life coach to a young adult.

- Make personal-care kits for residents at a senior center.

- Volunteer at a nearby wildlife refuge, nature preserve, or state park.

- Get the training required to take your pet to a hospital, nursing home, or convalescent center to brighten a patient's stay.

- Ask someone with a different ethnic background to share highlights of his or her life story.

- Go on a short-term missions trip through your church or a nonprofit.

- Write notes of personal encouragement to friends and acquaintances.

- Volunteer at a local museum, zoo, or aquarium.

If none of these ideas spark an idea, ask around or search online. Your church or civic group is a great place to start. The possibilities are endless. In any corner of your community, people need someone like you to make their lives a little brighter.

7. Can I (should I) have more than one purpose?

In Chapter 2 we looked at the importance and role of purpose in several key areas—our spirituality, vocation, families, creativity, and friendships. Since our lives are multidimensional, it follows that we will fulfill different purposes at different times and for different life roles. This is perfectly fine, as long as your purposes don't conflict with or contradict one another.

IN ANY CORNER OF YOUR COMMUNITY, PEOPLE NEED SOMEONE LIKE YOU TO HELP MAKE THEIR LIVES A LITTLE BRIGHTER.

For example, Joel's newly identified mission is to help mentor young men and new fathers. At the same time, one of his ongoing goals is to continue improving his personal fitness level through regular exercise classes, daily walks, and cycling.

These don't conflict with or contradict one another; in fact, each supports the other and brings balance and effectiveness to Joel's life and outreach. The key is to keep your purposes as simple and integrated as possible to avoid the frazzle of having a hodgepodge of passions that compete with one another.

8. What is my True North?

So far our questionnaire has dealt mostly with goals, desires, and dreams, which is a great start. Whether they are temporal or long-lasting, pursuing these passions can help you become a better person and do more good with each passing day.

Still, you may not have yet determined the *one, overarching life purpose* that will guide everything else in your life, including your peripheral goals, desires, and dreams. Most successful people I know have determined a True North for themselves—something that reflects an unchangeable, uncompromising value that will guide them all their days. Quite often this overarching life purpose is formed around one's spiritual beliefs, which most regard as vital to one's life today, tomorrow, and through eternity. It is their essential purpose in life, with all other dreams and desires (such as Joel's commitment to physical fitness or your desire for more schooling) complementing an overarching life purpose—their True North.

KEEP YOUR PURPOSES AS SIMPLE AND INTEGRATED AS POSSIBLE.

Our Creator made us with a deep-seated spiritual dimension that has both present-day and eternal implications. French physicist and philosopher Blaise Pascal put it this way: "There was once in man a true happiness ... which he in vain tries to fill from all his surroundings.... But these are all inadequate, because the infinite abyss can only be filled by an infinite and immutable object, that is to say, only by God Himself."[17]

DETERMINE TO LIVE IN A WAY THAT ACKNOWLEDGES GOD'S POWER, LOVE, AND AUTHORITY AND ALLOWS YOU TO DELIGHT IN HIS PRESENCE.

The God-shaped hole in our hearts is a void that will leave us floundering, incomplete, and unfulfilled until we invite God to fill it with himself. When we decide to partner with God, our True North begins to take shape and make sense. The Westminster Shorter Catechism, developed centuries ago to help teach key scriptural principles, describes mankind's True North in its very first question:

- **Question:** What is the chief end of man?

- **Answer:** Man's chief end is to glorify God and to enjoy him forever.[18]

It's difficult, perhaps impossible, to come up with a better definition of spiritual purpose. "Chief end" refers to our overarching purpose. God placed us on earth with a True North in mind—that we live today to glorify (honor) and enjoy him forever. For those who acknowledge and love him, it's a purpose with a promise!

While this God-awareness addresses primarily the spiritual aspect of our lives, it also forms an unmatchable creed to guide the entirety of one's life:

> *Because God's primary purpose for me is to honor and enjoy him each day, I determine to live in a way that acknowledges his power, love, and authority and allows me to delight in his presence. This is my personal True North, my most essential life purpose.*

If you genuinely believe the statement above, you won't go wrong making this your uncompromising primary purpose that covers and influences all of your supporting purposes. You'll also more wisely choose goals and dreams that honor and complement your primary purpose, as well as recognize flawed or weak ideas that do not contribute toward that end.

■ ■ ■

As we conclude this chapter, I encourage you to take a break for a few days, then come back and carefully review the concepts and self-assessments you've engaged with here. Take further notes of what stands out to you, and as you assess your strengths, successes, passions, and desires for the future, meditate on one more all-important question:

> *In light of my commitment to honor God by making a positive difference in my own life and in the lives of others, what one action point can I take this week to identify and live out my purpose?*

Your answers, followed by self-disciplined action, are going to make a huge difference—in your world, in your community, in your family, and in your soul.

"THE PURPOSES OF A PERSON'S HEART ARE DEEP WATERS, BUT ONE WHO HAS INSIGHT DRAWS THEM OUT."

—Proverbs 20:5

Activities *and* Exercises *to* Sharpen Your Focus

Throughout the preceding pages, you have been given plenty to think about as you consider the next steps in your life. And you have been asked many questions to reflect on to stimulate your brainstorming and dreaming.

In the following pages, I want to give you even more activities to prompt your thinking and help you pinpoint your path forward. Write your responses in your journal or in the spaces provided here.

My hope is that these questions will take you a giant step toward the most intentional and fulfilling life you've ever experienced.

Understanding Yourself

A brighter future awaits anyone who stops letting past choices and disappointments write their script. The following exercises will help you better understand yourself and identify the obstacles that are in your way—and boost your confidence that you have the power to clear them and move on.

Activities I loved to do when I was younger:

_____

_____

_____

_____

My reasons for stopping those things:

_____

_____

_____

_____

Activities that would make me happy now if money, time, and the approval of others were not obstacles:

_____

_____

_____

_____

_____

Possible reasons why I am alive on Planet Earth (Hint: gifts and talents you possess that the world needs):

_____

_____

_____

_____

_____

_____

Excuses I've made for not pursuing my dreams and purpose:

_____

_____

_____

_____

What I fear it would cost to boldly follow my dreams:

_____

_____

_____

Steps I can take today in the direction of my dreams:

_____

_____

_____

_____

Things I can do in the next year (and in the next five, ten, or twenty years) to stop sitting on the sidelines of my life and play the game with intentional purpose:

_____

_____

_____

_____

_____

My response to anyone (including myself) who says I can't achieve all this and more:

_____

_____

_____

_____

_____

Using *Your* Resources *for a* Reason

An important aspect of finding purpose in life centers on the word *stewardship*. It's not a term we use much anymore. Stewardship means different things to different people: Some think of a building campaign when they hear the word, while others think it means living frugally or getting out of debt.

In Scripture, stewardship means having temporary supervision over someone else's assets. And this isn't limited to financial assets but also includes talents and time. Each person on earth has been given certain *resources for a reason*.

God is the one who gives us a purpose—and the resources to achieve that purpose. He has entrusted us with money, intellect, energy, creativity, and other privileges that allow us to complete our divine calling. Our assignment and opportunity is to discover

> "AS EACH HAS RECEIVED A GIFT, USE IT TO SERVE ONE ANOTHER, AS GOOD STEWARDS OF GOD'S VARIED GRACE: WHOEVER SPEAKS, AS ONE WHO SPEAKS ORACLES OF GOD; WHOEVER SERVES, AS ONE WHO SERVES BY THE STRENGTH THAT GOD SUPPLIES—IN ORDER THAT IN EVERYTHING GOD MAY BE GLORIFIED THROUGH JESUS CHRIST."
>
> −1 Peter 4:10-11 ESV

this purposeful destiny and to utilize our resources wisely and fully as we pursue it with passion.

What God-given resources do you currently possess (talents, skills, possessions, influence, and so on)?

_____

_____

_____

_____

_____

_____

How have the experiences in your life—positive and negative—prepared you to be a wise steward? What difficult lessons and delightful lessons have you learned along the way?

_____

_____

_____

_____

_____

_____

_____

What are some specific ways you can more fully use your "resources for a reason" as you live with your purpose in mind?

_____

_____

_____

_____

_____

_____

_____

Listening *to* Feedback

When I was a student at Seattle Pacific University, I knew I wanted a career in a helping profession, but I wasn't sure which specific field I should pursue. I was seeking my purpose in life.

Several people offered ideas and guidance, but one person in particular gave me a powerful nudge that I remember vividly after four decades. A highly respected professor of psychology, Dr. Ruth Alexander, remarked after a meeting in her office, "Gregg, I believe you have the talent and temperament to be a skilled psychologist. I want you to consider pursuing a career in that field."

As if to add an exclamation point to her affirmation, Dr. Alexander walked over to her jam-packed bookshelves, pulled out several psychology books, and handed them to me. "I want you to have these as you begin to build your own library," she said.

I still have those books on my shelf! And I took Dr. Alexander's encouragement to heart, eventually choosing to become a psychologist.

We all need wise, respected people in our lives who will offer insight and counsel at strategic times. That's because others often recognize things about us that we don't, and they can offer ideas we didn't think of ourselves. As Proverbs 15:22 tells us, "Plans fail for lack of counsel, but with many advisers they succeed."

Reach out to people you trust and ask for their guidance as you ponder your future. Take note and look for patterns when someone pays you a compliment or makes an observation about you. Hearing what others notice about you might reinforce some of the passions you've already been following.

Who among your circle of friends and acquaintances can you call upon for input and counsel?

_____

_____

_____

_____

_____

_____

_____

When will you take the step of asking for advice—and how will you do it?

_____

_____

_____

_____

_____

_____

Giving *Yourself* Gifts

The process of clarifying your purpose can be confusing and stressful, so it's important to take good care of yourself along the way. Take some time to reflect on the kinds of gifts that only you can provide for yourself ... which might include these:

The Gift of Contentment

It's a well-known axiom that contentment can't be bought. True contentment has nothing to do with what you have or don't have. Proof lies in the fact that unhappy people are found on every rung of the economic ladder. Deep-down contentment has everything to do with emotional and spiritual well-being and is not dependent upon any possession, job title, or other external factor.

What one thing can you do this week to create more contentment in your life?

_____

_____

_____

_____

The Gift of Growth

Other people can provide encouragement and role-modeling as you seek a new direction for yourself—but the motivation and actual change can only come from within you. Look for ways to maximize your talents and lessen your shortcomings. The aim is not perfection but to reach your full potential. The gift of change-for-the-better is a blessing to yourself and everyone around you.

What is one growth area you would like to concentrate on in the coming months?

_____

_____

_____

_____

_____

The Gift of Forgiveness

While this may sound like a lofty ideal, forgiveness is, in fact, quite practical. You needn't be superspiritual to pull it off. A common misconception is that to forgive someone is to let them "get away" with something, to call offensive or hurtful behavior "okay" when it plainly wasn't. The truth is, forgiveness means choosing to cancel old emotional debts—and free yourself to get away with your heart intact, able to enjoy whatever comes next. In short, forgiveness frees you from embittered feelings and clears debris from the road ahead.

Think of one person you need to forgive. What are some steps you will take to go about this?

_____

_____

_____

_____

The Gift of Letting Go

Equally important is letting go of anything that is holding you back and weighing you down. It might be an emotional setback you encountered this past year, a promising relationship that ended badly, or a job prospect that didn't come through. Healing begins when we accept what is and what is not, learn from our past experiences, and look forward to the future with renewed hope.

What do you need to let go of to find freedom to move forward with joy and enthusiasm?

_____

_____

_____

_____

_____

_____

In your journal or a notebook, write out your thoughts and feelings about letting go of these things. Next, turn the page—literally and figuratively—by tearing it up and throwing it away, or doing whatever it takes to help you drop old baggage and cross the threshold into new possibilities.

The Gift of Less Worry

There is no end to things we might worry about: job security, tight finances, health concerns, political unrest, and relationship uncertainty. Anxiety is a wet blanket the world throws over you and the people you love. Nothing undermines inner peace faster than entertaining fear over some future event that may or may not ever happen. It causes you to miss the pleasures in the present moment and pass up purposeful opportunities in the future.

What is your biggest worry right now? How can you address it to put the concern in proper perspective?

_____

_____

_____

_____

_____

_____

The Gift of Gumption

Gumption is an old-fashioned word that means guts, bravery, or courage. Before another day goes by, take a deep breath and commit to one more tangible action that will move you in the direction of your dreams. Introspection and resolution are only profitable if they lead you to be bold and make real changes. This is the time to summon up all your gumption and go for it.

What one practical action can you take today to align with your purpose and move toward your envisioned life?

_____

_____

_____

_____

_____

_____

■ ■ ■

Too many years of lacking a strong sense of purpose may have hijacked your imagination, causing it to forecast only dull and dreary outcomes. This state of mind can easily misinterpret setbacks as failures, and obstacles as dead ends. As you journey toward your new purpose, it's inevitable that adversity will come to try to deter you from taking decisive steps forward.

In 1 Chronicles 28:20, we read that when King David charged his son Solomon with building a temple for the Lord, he said, "Be strong and courageous and do it. Do not be afraid and do not be dismayed, for the LORD God, even my God, is with you. He will not leave you or forsake you" (ESV). That statement reminds me of the Nike slogan that tells athletes to "Just do it." This is the spirit in which we need to put our plans and vision into action and to stare down any obstacle that comes our way—no excuses; just do it. The source of our courage is the fact that God will never leave us or forsake us.

"THE LORD HIMSELF GOES BEFORE YOU AND WILL BE WITH YOU; HE WILL NEVER LEAVE YOU NOR FORSAKE YOU. DO NOT BE AFRAID; DO NOT BE DISCOURAGED."

–Deuteronomy 31:8

Notes

1   Diane K. Osbon, ed., *Reflections on the Art of Living: A Joseph Campbell Companion* (New York: HarperPerennial, 1995), 24.

2   Quoted in Victor Perton, *Optimism: The How and Why* (Melbourne, Australia: The Centre for Optimism, 2022), 102.

3   Kozo Tanno et al., "Associations of Ikigai as a Positive Psychological Factor with All-Cause Mortality and Cause-Specific Mortality among Middle-Aged and Elderly Japanese People: Findings from the Japan Collaborative Cohort Study," *Journal of Psychosomatic Research* 67, no. 1 (July 2009): 67–75.

4   Dan Buettner, *Thrive: Finding Happiness the Blue Zones Way* (Washington, DC: National Geographic Society, 2010).

5   Patrick Hill and Nicholas Turiano, "Purpose in Life as a Predictor of Mortality across Adulthood," *Psychological Science* 25, no. 7 (July 2014): 1482–86.

6   Bruce W. Smith et al., "The Role of Resilience and Purpose in Life in Habituation to Heat and Cold Pain," *Journal of Pain* 10, no. 5 (May 1, 2009): 493–500.

7   Patricia A. Boyle et al., "Effect of a Purpose in Life on Risk of Incident Alzheimer Disease and Mild Cognitive Impairment in Community-Dwelling Older Persons," *Archives of General Psychiatry* 67, no. 3 (March 2010): 304–10.

8   Steve Jobs, "'You've Got to Find What You Love,' Jobs Says," June 14, 2005. *Stanford: News. https://news.stanford.edu /2005/06/14/jobs-061505/.*

9   Frederick Buechner, *Wishful Thinking* (New York: Harper & Row, 1973), 95.

10   Zameena Mejia, "Nearly 9 out of 10 Millennials Would Consider Taking a Pay Cut to Get This," updated June 28, 2018. *CNBC Make It: The Definitive Guide to Business. https://www.cnbc.com/2018/06/27/nearly-9-out-of-10 -millennials-would-consider-a-pay-cut-to-get-this.html.*

11   "Cartoon Coffee Break: Man's Search for Meaning," *Pen2Print Services. https://www.pen2print.org/2020/04 /cartoon-coffee-break-mans-search-for.html* (July 20, 2022).

12   Edward Jones and Age Wave, *The Four Pillars of the New Retirement: What a Difference a Year Makes*, June 2021. *Edward Jones. https://www.edwardjones.com/sites/default /files/acquiadam/2021-06/Four-Pillars-US-Report-June -2021.pdf*, 13.

13   Charles Schulz, *Peanuts*, March 15, 1981. *https://www .gocomics.com/peanuts/1981/03/15.*

14 Dhruv Khullar, "Finding Purpose for a Good Life. But Also a Healthy One," January 1, 2018. *New York Times: The Upshot.* *https://www.nytimes.com/2018/01/01/upshot/finding-purpose-for-a-good-life-but-also-a-healthy-one.html.*

15 Aaron Earls, "Americans' Views of Life's Meaning and Purpose Are Changing," April 6, 2021. *Lifeway Research.* *https://lifewayresearch.com/2021/04/06/americans-views-of-lifes-meaning-and-purpose-are-changing.*

16 Richard Swenson, *A Minute of Margin* (Colorado Springs: NavPress, 2003), reflection 175.

17 Blaise Pascal, *Pensées* (Mineola, NY: 2018), section VII, Morality and Doctrine, 113.

18 G. I. Williamson, *The Westminster Shorter Catechism for Study Classes*, second ed. (Phillipsburg, NJ: P&R Publishing), 1.

Image Credits

MORE RESOURCES FROM DR. GREGORY L. JANTZ

Unmasking Emotional Abuse

Six Steps to Reduce Stress

Ten Tips for Parenting
the Smartphone Generation

Five Keys to Dealing
with Depression

Seven Answers for Anxiety

Five Keys to Raising Boys

Freedom From Shame

Five Keys to Health and Healing

40 Answers for Teens'
Top Questions

When a Loved One Is Addicted

Social Media and Depression

Rebuilding Trust after
Betrayal

How to Deal with Toxic People

The Power of Connection

Why Failure Is Never Final

Find Your Purpose in Life

www.hendricksonrose.com